Secrets in the Rocks

Five Astounding Tales of People Solving Mysteries Beneath Our Feet

Nury Vittachi

Illustrations by Step Cheung

Contents

THE GIRL WHO FOUND A FLYING DRAGON

LITTLE MARY SEEMED TO BE destined for nothing but an early death.

She was born in a very poor family in the UK a little over 200 years ago. They had very little to eat and the only home they could afford was on the edge of the sea, near a dangerous cliff. No one else wanted to live there.

One by one, all her siblings had died except her brother Joseph. Her father, Richard Anning, a carpenter, was sick and dying, too.

The home of the Anning family was not just damp, but sometimes flooded so badly that they needed to climb out of an upstairs window to avoid drowning.

So Mary would leave her home and explore the cliffs, which contained some beautiful patterned rocks — although

the cliff walls were very crumbly, and there were sometimes landslides which killed visitors.

Her chances of survival were very low.

Then her father finally died and the last three members of the family realized that they did not have enough money to survive.

The local church gave Mary and her mother and brother cash to buy food, and taught the children how to read and write. This bought them some time and gave them hope.

But it turned out that the lethal seaside cliff where they lived would save their lives!

The strange, patterned rocks turned out to be fossils: remains of prehistoric animals or plants, preserved in rock. Mary and her mother and brother searched for fossils and made a little money selling them to collectors and museums.

In those days, the world's top science community was a group of men in the UK, mostly churchmen. They arranged for her fossils to be displayed and raised money for the poor family.

They were wise to put their trust in the Annings. One day Mary found some big fossils of animals that few people had ever seen before.

One of them was put into a museum under the name "Flying Dragon". It was an ancient dinosaur with huge, bat-like wings. (Today we call these creatures pterosaurs: dinosaur-era creatures which could fly like birds.)

Mary and her best friend, a little dog called Tray, also found the first ichthyosaur: a creature which is shaped like a dolphin but is an ancient swimming reptile with sharp teeth.

Her life changed. The girl grew up strong and healthy and she also found the first complete plesiosaurus, a large sea reptile that looks like the legendary "Loch Ness monster".

Then one day, while she was hunting, there was a huge landslide. It narrowly missed Mary — but killed her dog Tray. She was sad, but had suffered many losses of loved ones in her life. She thanked God for the time she did have with her dog — and then went back to work.

By the time Mary Anning was 27, she had saved enough money to buy a little home with a shop-front window where the fossils could be displayed.

She grew up to become one of the most famous fossil-finders in the world. Her little shop is still there. If you visit the UK, you can visit it. It is now called the Lyme Regis Museum, and is well worth a visit.

THE BOY WHO WENT SEARCHING FOR GIANTS

A SIX-YEAR-OLD BOY CALLED GEORGES loved puzzles. But not just the brainteasers that you find in newspapers or books.

He loved real life puzzles.

When an illusionist came to his town in France and did a series of magic tricks, little Georges Cuvier sat down with paper and pencil and worked out how the man had fooled everyone.

The family lived in the countryside and the boy spent many hours exploring nature with his mother.

And that's where he found the biggest puzzles of all: why was the world like it was? Why were there so many strange and wonderful animals and plants? And why were there so many stories told about giants and dragons and amazing creatures like that?

In Europe, archeologists said they had dug up the bones of giant men, who were even taller than the oldest, highest trees in the village.

What happened to the giants? Why had they died out?

As Georges Cuvier grew older, he started to sketch flowers and animals, and by the time he was 12, he was an expert naturalist.

Now all this happened in France in the 1700s, when only rich children received serious teaching. A wealthy nobleman noticed Georges' skill and paid for him to have a good education.

As an adult, Georges became a professor and decided to investigate the giants and other strange animals.

He realized that the fossil bones of the "giants" were not from humans at all. They were the bones of other big animals, such as elephants, and prehistoric creatures, such as mastodons.

This in itself was surprising, as there were no elephants in that part of Europe.

He found other fossils too, which seemed to belong to animals that were totally unknown!

One of the strangest things that ended up on his work table was a selection of parts of a creature that looked like a large reptile, but had large bat-like wings, and a beak with sharp teeth. (Less than 30 years later, little Mary Anning, who we met in the previous story, would find a related skeleton which would go on display as the "Flying Dragon".)

But Georges Cuvier's real contribution to science was an extraordinary idea — if you studied the shape of fossil bones and compared them to the shape of bones of living creatures, you could learn about the past, and how creatures were created or evolved.

And when he put all his findings together, he made a mind-blowing discovery.

We live in a world in which mammals, such as humans, dominate. But before that, there existed an entirely different world, right here, in which a completely different group of creatures, reptile-like animals, were dominant!

Georges Cuvier had discovered the world of the dinosaurs.

Today, this Frenchman is sometimes called "the father of paleontology".

But it's worth remembering that he started down the track to fame walking through the same forests that other people had walked, but being curious enough to ask questions no one had yet asked.

He disproved the tales about giants, but became a "giant of science" himself.

LOVE, ROCKS AND THE FIRST DINOSAUR

MARY'S MOTHER DIED SOON after she was born. The toddler was given to a couple who had no children of their own.

This worked out well, because they gave her lots of love, but also educated her, even though in the UK in those days (the early 1800s), only boys were usually allowed to go to school.

She was good at art, and when she was in her twenties, her adoptive father gave her some bones (some people thought they were bones of a giant, see the previous story) to draw for a fossil expert he knew.

By the time she was 27, Mary Morland was fascinated by paleontology, and when a new book came out about rocks and fossils, she bought a copy and took it with her on a train journey.

Now just hold that thought for a moment.

A little distance away lived the fossil expert whom her father knew.

William Buckland was single professor aged 40. He knew there was a young woman who shared his interests, and he decided to look for her. To occupy his mind on the train journey, he took a newly published book on rocks and fossils.

You can guess what happened.

The two ended up in the same carriage, holding identical books. Love blossomed.

Mary and Will got married and spent a year on honeymoon, visiting famous rock formations and fossil experts.

The Bucklands had a great career as paleontologists, and worked well as a team.

For example, one day, explorers saw strange, fossilized scrape marks in ancient rocks. What sort of beast could make those marks?

William puzzled over the problem way past midnight. At 2 a.m., he had an idea.

"Mary," he said, "Use flour to make a paste, and then lay it over the kitchen table." And then he opened the back door and went out into the night. Why? Where was he going?

But she knew her husband well enough to trust that he must have had a brainwave.

He returned with a tortoise from the garden, and placed it on the table. It moved across the floury paste — and made the exact same marks. They now knew the marks were the fossilized tracks of an ancient tortoise.

When William was an old man, he used his knowledge of rocks to play a final joke. He told the gravedigger that he wanted to be buried in a certain place.

After his death, they discovered that the spot had just a few inches of soil, below which was a huge slab of Jurassic rock. It was impossible to dig there.

But they were determined to follow his wishes. They used explosives to make a hole big enough for the grave.

Mary died the following year.

If you look up the name of the very first dinosaur to be given a scientific name, you'll find Megalosaurus bucklandii. Can you see what's hidden in the second part of that name? Yes, it's the family name of William and Mary Buckland.

THE BUG BOY SOLVES A HUGE MYSTERY

THE BUG BOY WAS PUZZLED. His family had no money, so his playground was the area of woods and fields around his humble home in Switzerland.

Yet the things he found outdoors did not make sense.

Rocks from one mountain were found on top of another. Fish fossils were discovered far away from any sea. And natural features like hills and cliffs were often striped with straight lines that seemed to point to something. But what?

The boy's name was Louis Agassiz, and he was 10 years old. We call him the bug boy because he often took creatures home with him. He would keep caterpillars in jars and watch carefully to see how they turned into butterflies.

Then his parents gave him some big news. They had saved enough money to send him to school for the first time — but the school was far away.

He was sad to leave them, but knew that this was an opportunity he should take. He also missed his brother, Auguste, who was not interested in bugs, but was fascinated by machines — especially tiny ones such as the insides of watches.

As Louis Agassiz grew into a young teenager, he did not lose his love of nature, and soon had a whole, live tree in the room where he lived — and made sure that there were birds and bugs in the tree, so he could study them.

I don't think most modern children would like a tree full of birds and bugs in their bedroom!

When he was fifteen, his parents told him that he had to stop studying and get a job — that was the normal age to finish education in those days, the 1820s.

But the boy begged to be allowed to go on studying, and the parents, who were a preacher and his wife, saved up more money and let him carry on.

Louis Agassiz went to study mountains and built himself a hut on top of a glacier — a river of ice.

There he studied the way that glaciers moved rocks and fossils around, and he and his colleagues found the answer to a huge puzzle. An unimaginably big glacier, an ice sheet, must have covered many countries in the past. It would have covered Britain and most of Europe. And that's why so many things had moved, with rocks and bones from one area found in other areas, miles away.

The bug boy had discovered the Ice Age.

Many years later, other scientists investigated this idea, and found that the theory was right. More than a quarter of the landmasses of the planet had been covered with a huge sheet of ice, 20,000 years ago.

Louis became famous. But so did his brother, in a different way. Sometimes you might see advertisements for a famous watch brand called Longines. That's the company of the bug-boy's brother.

Their parents, in their little church in the hills, must have been proud of both of them.

THE WOMAN WHO SAW DEEP INTO THE EARTH

LOTS OF PEOPLE LIKE interesting stones and pebbles, but Inge loved extremely big rocks: she loved mountains.

One day when she was in her mid-teens she was sitting on the sofa with her mother and sister on a Sunday morning.

She felt the ground beneath her feet tremble and then everything shook — the seats, the walls, and even the ceiling. The lamp above her head swung from side to side.

Her father rushed into the room. "It was an earthquake," he said.

And so, Inge Lehman, a girl born in 1888 in Denmark, became interested in the biggest rock of all: the planet Earth, third rock from the sun.

Twenty years after experiencing that earthquake, Inge became a seismologist.

That means she was an expert in measuring movements under the ground — the shaking that accompanies earthquakes, but that also happens in less disruptive ways at other times.

Inge and her colleagues realized that if you collected a lot of detailed records about earthquakes you could work out a surprisingly large amount of information about what was deep inside the Earth — deeper than any explorer could reach.

She spent months studying the data and realized that 250 kilometers under our feet, something changed. Earth had a different texture that far down.

Scientists today call this the Lehmann Discontinuity, naming it after its discoverer.

But then Inge Lehmann found something even more interesting. Until then, scientists had believed that the center of the Earth was a huge molten ball.

She studied the way that trembles and shakes ran through the planet and came to a different conclusion. The core of the planet had two sections. The outer core was molten, like a superheated liquid, but right at the center of the world, there was an incredibly hot, solid ball of metal.

Scientists checked her results and realized that they explained the data perfectly. People were amazed that a woman working in an office on the surface of the world could detect what was in the planet's center!

When Inge was an old woman, she spent her summers quietly in a cottage away from the city. Once a visitor came to see her — and was amazed to find that Inge had chosen a room at the top of the house for herself, and climbed up a ladder every night to get there.

Even at the age of 70, mountain-lover Inge Lehmann still loved climbing.

She died at the age of 104 in 1993.

If one hot day you can become powerfully aware that the sun is a fiery ball above your head, take a moment to remember the Danish scientist who discovered that there is another fiery hot ball beneath our feet.

KEEP READING

READING ABOUT THE LIVES of scientists and other discoverers adds to our store of knowledge, but we hope also leads us towards something much greater, which is wisdom.

This book is part of a series, which we hope you'll enjoy reading, and will spur you on to do your own scientific research.

The creators of this book wish you success in your explorations.

THE YOUNG SCIENTISTS SERIES

Book 1: SECRETS IN THE ROCKS
Five Astounding Tales of People Solving Mysteries Beneath Our Feet

Book 2: FABULOUS PHYSICS
Five Amazing Stories of People Who Solved Nature's Puzzles

Book 3: MAGICAL MATHEMATICS
Five Astonishing Stories of People Who Did Miracles with Numbers

Book 4: BREAKERS OF BARRIERS
Five Stunning Stories of People Demolishing Walls to Make History

Book 5: SCIENTIFIC PIONEERS
Five Incredible Tales of People Who Helped Develop the Scientific Method

Book 6: THE AMAZING QUANTUM
Five Awesome Stories of People Who Made a Revolution in Physics

Book 7: THE SCIENCE OF HUMANITY
Five Fascinating Stories of People Who Helped Us Understand Ourselves

Book 8: WOMEN OF DISCOVERY
Five Super Stories of Fabulous Females Who Made Scientific History

Book 9: THE INVENTOR'S SPARK
Five Marvelous Stories of People Who Helped Shape the Modern World

Book 10: ADVANCES IN ALCHEMY
Five Startling Stories of Chemistry and Biology

Book 11: THE CALL OF THE STARS
Five Wonderful Stories of People Looking to the Heavens

Book 12: MYSTERIES OF NATURE'S LAWS
Five Striking Stories of People Investigating the Deepest Puzzles of Reality

Published by

WS Education, an imprint of
World Scientific Publishing Co. Pte. Ltd.
5 Toh Tuck Link, Singapore 596224
USA office: 27 Warren Street, Suite 401-402, Hackensack, NJ 07601
UK office: 57 Shelton Street, Covent Garden, London WC2H 9HE

National Library Board, Singapore Cataloguing in Publication Data
Name(s): Vittachi, Nury, 1958– | Cheung, Step, illustrator.
Title: Secrets in the rocks : five astounding tales of people solving mysteries beneath our feet / author, Nury Vittachi ; illustrator, Step Cheung.
Other title(s): Young scientists series ; 1.
Description: Singapore : World Scientific Publishing Co Pte Ltd, 2017.
Identifier(s): OCN 969701927 | ISBN 978-981-3221-32-1 (paperback)
Subject(s): LCSH: Paleontologists--Juvenile literature. | Scientists--Juvenile literature. | Paleontology--Juvenile literature. | Science--Juvenile literature.
Classification: DDC 560.922--dc23

British Library Cataloguing-in-Publication Data
A catalogue record for this book is available from the British Library.

All royalties received will be channelled to the National Book Development Council of Singapore (NBDCS) as a gift from the author.

First published 2017
Reprinted 2018

Printed in Singapore